On This Earth

On This Earth

Poems by

Barbara DiMauro

© 2025 Barbara DiMauro. All rights reserved.
This material may not be reproduced in any form, published,
reprinted, recorded, performed, broadcast,
rewritten, or redistributed without
the explicit permission of Barbara DiMauro.
All such actions are strictly prohibited by law.

Cover design by Shay Culligan
Cover photo by Jen Dries
Author photo by Harold Shapiro

ISBN: 978-1-63980-722-2
Library of Congress Control Number: 2025936483

Kelsay Books
502 South 1040 East, A-119
American Fork, Utah 84003
Kelsaybooks.com

for my granddaughter Geetha
I will always love you

Contents

The Physiology of Grief	13
The Little Room	15
The Forgiveness Factor	17
That Place	18
Unzippered	19
Fractures	20
Disappearance	21
Sinister Spaces	22
Anywhere But Here	24
Bones	25
If I Could Speak to My Heart	27
Placebo Effects	28
All Those Years	30
Sleeping on Snow	31
The Price of Passion	32
Trail Magic	33
The Gratitude of Houseplants	34
Sea Mist and Salt	35
Singing like an idiot	36
Denali	37
A Walk in the Cemetery	38
On This Earth	39
The End of the World	40
Unearthly Possessions	41
The Field of Lost Love	42
Sister	44
Notes on the Pursuit of Joy	45
Perpetual Motion	46
Women in Pink	47
Hope	48
Apologies	49
Confession	50

Safety Redefined	51
Reinvention	52
The Bubble Lady	53
Opinions	55
Things I Thought I Could Not Live Without	56
Sleepless	57
The Swallows Return	58
Something in the Water	59
June's Long Days	60
Meeting Up with Second Chance	61
Twilight	62
Signs of Life	63
So Many Ways to Hide	64
History	65
Tethered	66
Unrecorded Lives	67

My contemplation is an excruciation only because it is also a joy.

—Simone de Beauvoir

The Physiology of Grief

For some it starts in the throat,
the passageway through which
all words travel
but they travel listlessly now
syllables tangled on the
filaments of disbelief
and when they finally reach the mouth
there is no sound but keening,
which is the only way to describe
what is happening to you.

For others it's the brain;
grief crashes its way across
the frontal cortex and
into a landscape of gray and white
and turns you into someone
who has profound difficulty
thinking or acting or planning
though you *do* notice that everyone
around you is wearing funeral clothing
so you become vaguely aware that
the life you once had
is over.

Of course there's the heart
which grief strikes like
a lightning bolt,
and there's already enough electrical activity
transpiring in that organ
to jumpstart an inferno.

But what you feel in your chest
are the staccato beats of a drummer
who is failing miserably
to synchronize with the band.
Then pain announces itself
and you feel faint as well.

Suddenly the sweetest relief
washes over you as you realize
you are about to die.
You close your eyes and pray
to the gods and goddesses and
the witnesses nearby:
Please don't revive me.
Why should you?
For what?
For whom?

The Little Room

For a year I lived there,
solitude the most reasonable
ambition I'd ever had.
So much happened
in that little room,
not just the midnight blue curtains
that I hung on one small window
facing the busy intersection
or the thrift shop furniture that
that I dragged from around the corner;
one wooden chair, a single bed frame,
an improvised desk, barely making it
through the door, creating a clutter
that belonged to no one else but me.

As I said, so much happened in that little room,
where I tried relentlessly
to sequester myself from my own species
and suffered the outrage of my fate.
Safely behind a locked door
questions hovered in the air
as if they had arrived by courier
with an urgent message:
What is it that I owe myself?
Where do I go from here?
And when I realized these questions
came directly off my own tongue,
no longer tied, and formed a voice,
no longer muffled,
I began to respond in run-on sentences,
my words no longer trapped
in the basement of my brain.

I had so much to say and
I knew the answers
to every question
and for the first time in my life
I was an A student
and no one ever again would claim
to be more of an expert than I was
about the woman in the little room
where so much happened.

The Forgiveness Factor

I'm standing at the threshold
of forgiveness
but something pulls me back
with palpable force
and that sensation moving
through me just minutes before,
be it hope or resolve
evaporates like a winter breath
and I turn away from you completely,
drawing a line through your name,
remembering the exactness
of the wounds you inflicted
and marking the moment
as an occasion for mourning.

That Place

I went to that place
all sharp edges and dark corners,
dirt under my swaying foothold
glowing red,
silhouettes of stealthy assassins,
blood battering hard against my chest,
my spine tingling.
Oh yes, I wandered there
more than once
and when I started to miss the smell of
salt marshes at low tide, I never went back.
But I remember.

Unzippered

Oh that smooth glide of soft metal,
rising up to warm me, pulling me inward,
holding me tight against the elements,
whatever they may be.
I could be sung to sleep in that bundled safety,
never having to turn my sights inward,
well protected against the outward forces
that relentlessly sweet-talk me into unzipping
my coat of arms and freeing from hibernation
those howling larynx sounds
and when I do everyone can listen,
no reservations needed.
Some cheer me on, nodding their heads
in proud agreement; others feel
the lash and sting of well-deserved words
that will leave behind reminders like
surgical incisions in the shape
of an apology.

Fractures

Some of them never really go away
though it may appear that they've healed
so you live your life unreasonably happy
for a while
telling yourself it could have been much worse,
that you were lucky.
Then the residue of promise begins to dissolve
and it comes back,
not exactly pain, something nondescript,
like a shapeless shadow
and it's too deep so you can't grasp it
and rid yourself of it once and for all
and even that hand
whose comfort you once craved
can't make it go away.

Disappearance

I saw her in the grocery store,
a young girl about ten years old
but aware beyond her years
and no wonder
with her thick as brick eyeglasses
and what I gathered was a limp
from an early injury,
oh, nobody knows the strife
in her life, not even her mother
who walked ahead of her
on her cell phone the whole time
oblivious to her child's fear
of being noticed,
but I knew, I knew her well
stranger that she was to me
and when I finally was able to get up close
enough to meet her face to face
she regarded me angrily with eyes that shouted
Don't look at me! I'm trying to disappear!

Sinister Spaces

Not the dark littered alleys
of grunge and cigarettes
or the parking garages of late-night
silence where strangers lurk
with malicious intent.

No, it could be any room you enter,
maybe one with tall windows boasting sunshine
or another where a celebration of some sort
is in full swing, or any room, really
where humans gather
to unleash their humanness.

At first you're engaged
but soon the cold cement of reality
cracks wide open
and something feels very wrong,
like a collection of rare books
overturned in the rain.
With revulsion you notice that
behind the capped-toothed smiles
appalling words linger like
contagions in the air
leaving the taste of dirt on your tongue
and the banter that throbs all around you
leaves nothing to your imagination.
And you can bet your life
that not a single person
in the room would dare step into your shoes
and feel your despair on any given day,
you, a woman who still believes in
reparations for the sins of history
and that she can take back the night
on streets that belong to everyone.

Yes, this is a place
where certain common virtues don't exist
and people feast on the wounds
of 'the other' with unhindered glee.

What else to do but
scan the layout for means of escape,
tip-toe past that legendary beast of
ignorance and hatred,
hit the pavement
and run for your life?

Anywhere But Here

Anywhere but here,
that's what I was once thinking.
Were you? Ever?
Feigning interest
feigning presence
perhaps too often
and too much time
spent wanting only
to be a rock in a river
or a stone in a stream
solaced by cool clean
water rippling over me.

Those dreaded conversations,
the men, little boys concealed inside them,
the pontificating intellectuals at my table,
loneliness in crowded rooms,
between the sheets of lost desire
no keys for escape
no exit signs
time full-throttle
distorting and spinning
turning seconds into years
and me a hostage of my own tolerance.
Until something slow and silent
in me stirs, then, harsh, insistent
and *enough, enough* is what I hear as I walk away.

Bones

You took me far, I'll give you that,
you of unbleached beauty
stronger than concrete,
the architect of my life.

From the prima ballerina wannabe
who didn't know the difference
between a femur and a fibula
but could remain en pointe
longer than my classmates,
my small head filling up with fantasies
about life on a stage
(a brilliant substitution for real life)
to the wannabe athlete
lacing up my fancy sneakers
every day, crossing more finish lines
than I can count
running for my life if I'm honest
but by then I knew that my hip bone
was connected to my spinal vertebrae
and that I should grudgingly stick
it out through weeks of shin splints.

I knew too much really, but still
I stayed the distance
no pain no gain
keep on keeping on.
I know I should be grateful to you
for all those years
and maybe even apologetic
because I never wondered if I'd
gone too far or too fast or
if you could bear the weight of decades.

I'm sorry, but I wasn't counting on
being easily breakable or inflamed
(though I have every reason to be)
or measuring my pain with a shrinking yardstick.

How silly of me to think you were flawless,
that you would never crumble like a
citadel of centuries past,
that you would last forever
but only in the grave.

If I Could Speak to My Heart

If I could speak to my heart,
that mercurial muscle,
caged as it is by my ample chest
yet arbiter of life and death
and described by many as bleeding or broken,
but not by me, who has plenty
to say otherwise:
your wild thumping jolts me to my senses
when I prefer to be numb
and when your rhythm is off
all I can hear are the dissonant
notes of a frenzied song
and you require care
when I care about nothing
and your silence can be maddening
when I crave signs of life.
But there's not a thing I can do about you
my mercurial heart
but speak to you as I often do:
beat, beat,
not too long
but long enough.

Placebo Effects

I was hoping to get the *real thing*,
the life I always wished for.
All I had to do
was swallow the remedy that was offered
along with the lies I was told
and consent to a blindfold
that would grant me a glimpse
of a painless existence.
Some would call it mind-breaking work
or brainwashing at its best,
but I didn't care, at least not then.

I must have believed
that what I wanted badly enough
would be mine and everything
worth having I could keep;
that there would no longer be
onslaughts of strife
and words that would wound me
and grief I thought I wouldn't survive.

Well as it turns out, the remedy didn't take;
in fact there *was* no remedy.
There was no greener grass
or stairway to heaven
or dreams that came true,
only remnants of the magical thinking
that marked my childhood.
But it also turned out that
I did get the *real thing*,
not exactly what I expected
but I know now that expectation
has no kinship with reality.

What I got was an imperfect life,
a human one.
One that is weighty
with the cruelty of the world
but always close enough
to the source of love.

All Those Years

All those years
I hid behind a veil of anger,
drinking a daily dose
of vitriol, looking for someone
to bury my darkness in.
I was the enemy of my own kindness,
keeper of my own promise of exile,
but the lingering scent of regret
was left behind whenever
a chance at love was offered.

Sleeping on Snow

I dreamed I was sleeping
on snow but I wasn't cold.
I was alone in the
glacial dark of night,
somehow aware that
there would never be sunlight.
The bone bleached moon
wandered above me
beams bouncing off the
brilliant white
and when I opened my eyes
glitter like a thousand suns
across a boundless field
cast its light on me.
And in the dream I understood
that magnificence makes warm
the coldest place on earth.

The Price of Passion

You've done things you've never done before.
You've thought things you've never thought before.
People's words seem clumsy and hollow
and they don't apply to you;
there's only one voice you want to hear.
Your breathing seems to be originating
from somewhere foreign, not your lungs.
You don't eat.
You can't sleep.
You have fewer and fewer ordinary days.
Reality has become pinched into one sphere.
You're not yourself
and everyone around you knows it.
You know it.
And isn't it extraordinary to finally be alive?

Trail Magic

There's stillness here despite the gusty wind
and I wonder how that's possible.
The gem-like eyes of a red fox
stare me down from behind
a disheveled heap of fallen branches
then disappear.
Did I really see them?
The pain in my worn-out knees
vacates my body through
the soles of my feet and suddenly
I'm skipping.
An explosion of finches abandon
a Ponderosa pine and accompany me
to the next trailhead.
And what on earth is that creature gliding
above me from one tree to another?
Since when can squirrels fly?
A white tail deer scampers swiftly
across my path then fades into nowhere.
Where did she go?
My hair smells like evergreen perfume.
I am consoled and redeemed
and inspired all at once.
Now tell me,
if this isn't magic,
what is?

The Gratitude of Houseplants

You've lived with me for years,
my silent children,
your body rooted to
the place that suits you best.
I spare you lovingly
from the extremes of weather
and for that you offer me
cleaner air to breathe.
I gladly crouch low
or crane my neck
or climb a ladder
to keep you alive
and for that you show me
your beautiful veins,
purple, pink, yellow,
not all the colors of a rainbow,
but close.
You all want different things
at different times
and as my mouth grazes your foliage
I talk to you, a monologue of reassurance
that you'll always have what you need
and for that you speak to me
in your wordless language
with the flicker of a leaf
or a nod toward the light
or a bloom in my favorite color:
Thank you. Thank you.

Sea Mist and Salt

Sea mist and salt
overwhelm me,
wash me clean
and I become a better woman,
dwelling on the shore of wisdom,
and swimming in my own waters
and when my seaworn lips part
they speak nothing but the truth.

Singing like an idiot

in my car on my way
to a medical appointment
radio off
at the grocery store
ignoring the gawks
taking out the trash
with a throatful of Pink
my cacophonous voice rising
in the air with the cadence
of suspense
a special kind of noise pollution
I think the pigeons love it
I'm idiotic
I'm delirious
drunk on the smell of
rotted leaves and pollen
and skunk cabbage
Spring is arriving
and I am her voice

Denali

I felt I was fated to
write such a poem
but I couldn't do it.
Oftentimes I sat at my desk,
pen in hand
and oftentimes I failed dreadfully.
It's not a place
words can eloquently describe
and so I came to understand
that trying to do so
trivializes its very existence.
Instead of writing about what
you might see there,
what you might feel there
and how it might change your life,
I'll simply say that you should go there.
Look, listen, let it fill you up.
And then you'll understand.

This, finally, is the poem.

A Walk in the Cemetery

Bonaventure Cemetery
Savannah, Georgia

In a land of underground voices
and abbreviated biographies
on stone, the earth under my feet
expanding and contracting
like a multitude of sighs,
I walk the curving pathways
around the unfinished stories
of the famed and the ordinary:
poets and masons,
soldiers and lyricists,
bound to a unity of
endless time and place.

I feel at peace in this unearthly dwelling
where nothing happens but solemn footfalls
and coastal breezes that rouse the
dripping Spanish moss.
Where marble statues with intangible tears
mourn those who will never notice
the pink and purple magnolias
dressed in their finery
and beatifically adorning their graves.

On This Earth

On this earth
day breaks with shards of light.
Apples cling to bare branches.
Seagulls plow through
another winter.
A girl with pigtails encounters
the beginning of knowledge.
A dog smiles hello to his mistress.
Pink flamingos quiver on weed-laden lawns.
Clouds invade the horizon.
A woman in a supermarket is intent
on finding the best eggplant for the price.
A saxophonist releases his notes to the universe.

On this earth
sleepers disarm and surrender to the night.
They dream of fire and floods
and wars and hatred
but they wake and remember only
those things that keep them alive.

The End of the World

I imagine it often.
A thick dust, smoky gray,
making it hard to see.
A black outline
is all that's left of the sun.
Meteorites crash with reckless abandon,
at least I think that's what they are.
There are mountains of rubble everywhere
sinking into the hollowed-out earth.
The severed wings of birds
are scattered all over.
Trees are scorched to the root.
The smell is sickening and I shake off
the thought that it's human decay.

Every horror that exists in the world
has happened here,
can be seen and felt here.

And when I pull myself out
of this imaginary landscape
of ash and carnage
I realize that it isn't
the end of the world at all.
It is war.

Unearthly Possessions

Army dog tags draped over a mirror
a fistful of fur in a mason jar
a black velvet evening coat wrapped
in tissue paper
a diamond engagement ring
in a satin jewel pouch
a lone cordial glass
displayed in a china cabinet.
There's much more, believe me
the list is long.
Objects that never belonged to me
but are mine now
courtesy of sorrow.
I am their keeper
and I keep them well
as if I believe that
their rightful owners will someday
return to reclaim them.
Until then, I will remember.

The Field of Lost Love

I've always wondered
where love goes
when it dies.
Or perhaps it never dies
no matter how shattered it is
but survives beyond the grasp
of any explanation
living for years in every second,
waiting for another chance.

But where does it actually go?

To a battle-scarred library
in the humanities section,
kept alive by overhead fluorescents
but without a heart to reside in?
Perhaps it lingers in the stratosphere
with just enough oxygen to keep it alive,
doomed to nothingness,
an aftermath worse than a demon's embrace.
Or is it burned to ashes
but still smoldering,
sitting on a fireplace mantle
inside a forgotten urn,
its orange sparks unable to fly?

No, no, I can't comprehend
such fate.

Instead I imagine that it lives
in a boundless field of purple sage
and tall grasses
and goldenrod,
thriving on the elements of nature,
conjuring loss into possibility
and hinging on a temperate wind
that echoes what is left behind
but promises something
as seismic as a first kiss.

Sister

for Nancy

Who else but you
understands the grief in my gaze?
Who sees straight through my hysterical laughter?
Who forgives the acid and sword of my words
because their source is so familiar?
Who feels the weight that skulks beneath
my skin having lived with the same heaviness?
Who has memorized the etchings of my heart
because it is an exact replica of her own?
Who else but you?

Notes on the Pursuit of Joy

Hard won but possible,
you just have to know where to look
and when to walk away.

Craning your neck too far forward
can leave you gasping at the throat
of discontent
and leaning too close to a whisper
can mute the sound
of your own warnings.
Don't let the provocative expertise
of desire get in the way,
as things may look clearer
the greater the distance.

Sometimes opening your mouth wide
to the sky and tasting rain is all there is.

Perpetual Motion

I must admit that I was already bordering
on what would be considered old
before I understood that perpetual motion
will never suspend the passage of time.

Oh yes, I was once powered by adrenaline
petal to the metal
lunching while I drove
moored to a checklist of tasks
that I mistook for accomplishments
sleeping only when I had to
life careening past through murky windows
with nothing truly visible in any direction,
disregarding dreams of
noiseless daybreaks
and floating on the water
and exchanging bedlam for indolent days of bliss.

It took a while
but now I know
there's something to be said
for rerouting oneself from heavy traffic
and coasting in the breakdown lane,
continually amazed at how much there is to see.

Women in Pink

If I were viewing from above,
in a helicopter, say,
all I would glimpse is a sea of pink
unfurling for miles like a tidal wave
of flamingoes with cat-like ears.
But on the ground there's a different story,
one that's worthy of telling
but if you don't like the
personal and political intertwined
you don't have to listen.
It's the story of women
who knitted their way to Washington DC
with hands young and old
black, white, brown and yellow
and voices that carried the fury of generations
and feet that took them
to the front lines of the good fight.
It's the story of women
who move through a world
of blockades at every turn,
but with heads held high,
fearless, buoyant
powered by might,
onward they go.

Hope

Has hope lost its power
after being suffocated
and tossed around recklessly
for so long?
Did it die right in front of me
while I was preoccupied
with the crimes against nature
or the slow but steady decline
in the goodness of humanity?
Or was it while I watched—
for a split second—
two dolphins frolicking
silver on silver
in the rugged swells
of the Bering Sea,
a split second that changes everything?

Apologies

Too many are like fog,
ungraspable, diaphanous
rendered with lowered eyes
and platitudes
when what you most need
is the grit
of a loose tongue
that catapults words
to your wrecked heart
with the force of a grenade
and the gravity of
a landing on the moon.

Confession

Bless me father
for I have sinned
so let me say the
words you long to hear
while I suffocate in
this claustrophobic box
of fire and brimstone
and nod solemnly as you
dole out your just punishments
and finally I can escape and tear
the scarf off my luscious hair
and shake off all the lies I told you
and forge on with a life of
pride lust greed gluttony envy
but not until
I feed the two
stray cats in my neighborhood
and cook my family
their favorite dinner
and drive my elderly neighbor
to her medical appointment
and write a check
for a friend who needs it
and only then will I have time
to bow my head in prayer
and ask for forgiveness.

Safety Redefined

What safety once meant
no longer applies,
that thing we knew
backwards and forwards—
never the need for description—
because it lived in our bones
in the smiles on our faces
in the unfettered play of our children.

Safety in numbers?
Not today.
Safety within the hearth and home?
No longer.
Where to take asylum
is now as important a question as
what do I want to do with my life?

For me there's only this:
the hand on my shoulder
that will never abandon me.

Reinvention

You thought it would be
the hardest thing you would ever do
but as it turns out, it's effortless
as long as you loathe what you see
when you look in a mirror
and are ready to answer a call of discovery.

When the time comes you hardly
have to think about it
which I suppose is how it is with snakes,
who shed their skin in its entirety
when they outgrow it or when it's
old and worn out, which is quite clever
if not ingenious.

You tell yourself you can do it too
even though you may perish in a
wasteland of ambiguity.

Then one day you're no longer
that woman weeping in a restroom stall
or vomiting up the meal you just ate
or fighting for your life in the back seat of a car.
The name and photo on your license are still the same,
but you are no longer her.

The Bubble Lady

for Julia Vinograd
December 11th, 1943–December 5th, 2018

Polio and poverty didn't stop you—
couldn't stop you—
from writing seventy volumes of poetry,
seventy!
and releasing them in their living forms
to the archives of history.

Yet scandalously,
with the exception of your
own beloved Berkeley nation,
most people have never heard of you,
you, an icon of the sixties' cultural revolution,
you, the bubble lady of Telegraph Avenue!

You, in your black and yellow shiny beret,
adorned with a button that proclaimed
Weird and Proud,
blowing bubbles in peaceful protest
which you did nearly your whole life.

You took your passion for the homeless
and mentally ill to the streets,
(a woman after my own heart)
where you could always be found
in keen observance of the human condition,
taking notes in your head
and in the late evenings
placing them devotedly on paper
in your room at the Berkeley Inn.

I wish I had known you, though it feels like I do,
as I've lost myself in so many of your poems
we could have been sisters.
I picture us walking *The Ave* together
arm in arm, you in your legendary attire
and on this particular day
I'm the one who's blowing bubbles,
weird and proud and wanting
every millisecond of
this moment
this day
this place
to last a lifetime.

Opinions

Opinions. Mine.
How many? Many.
I might have lost a friend or two
over the useless cause of opinions.

They're unwinding in my gut
today, every day, whirring
in my hard head, a swarm of
facts drenched with passion
escaping with abandon
and looking for someone—
anyone—to sing them to
or hurl them at,
take your pick.

The art of Italian cuisine.
Why you shouldn't kill insects.
Politics, politics, more politics.
How best to deal with the onslaughts of age.
Hammering my points insistently
with my mouthful of rust.

I ask myself:
Am I a pontificating fool?
Why must I give expression to every indignation?
Are my opinions necessary
or all I have to offer?

I tell myself:
Shut up shut up shut up.
But I never do.
I'm not ready to die yet.

Things I Thought I Could Not Live Without

There are too many to name here
and at this point most of them should
be donated to a museum of antiquities.

They were things I coveted
for weeks, months
until I knew I could possess them,
until I could almost feel their somethingness
in my widened palms.
Things that had an expiration date,
at least for me,
things whose appeal swiftly wore out
like a shallow assumption,
things that failed to transform my life.

Why didn't I know that all I wanted
was a light so elegant it invents a sunrise
and a hand in mine, wet with saltwater?

Sleepless

It's 1am and sleep
is yanked away from me like
a stolen gift.
Oh, not again!

I keep my eyes closed in defiance
but still, jumbled thoughts and images
creep up from my unconscious
like a creature rising
from its ill-fitting sheath,
the perfect grist for the analyst's couch.
Why do you invade my night?

Hours pass and I'm still awake.
I take a sleeping pill
even though I know it won't
silence the tumult going on
behind my eyes, flailing
in and out of coherence,
beneath dusty layers of time and memory
and set on repeat in an endless loop.
Please let me sleep!

I don't sleep.

But when night is finally finished with me
and the first piece of dawn announces itself
through the threads of closed curtains,
I plant my feet firmly on the floor,
drawn to the day in front of me,
my eyes open wide to a waking life.

The Swallows Return

I wait for you every Spring
the first sighting
my melancholy
turned to pleasure
I hear you singing
and watch you play
your tiny bodies
darting and swooping
among my seagrasses
your seagrasses
and swaying along
with the oyster gray wind
you come every year
to the same place
my home
your home

Something in the Water

I watch them from a distance
teetering on the water's edge.
They fear something
but they can't say what.
They walk back and forth
back and forth,
then tentatively dip their toes in
and pull them out with a shriek,
scorched by a cool wave
of trepidation.

I wonder what flawed imaginings
they're struggling with:
a kingdom of mysteries beneath the sea
that portend tragedy?

I walk toward the ocean,
intent on showing them something,
but I can't say what.
I glide in and I float and swim and dive
and I'm farther and farther
away from shore
and I turn and watch them looking
out at me, transfixed
and I hope they see
the delicious ease of my movements
as I catch each wave
and I hope they understand
that if they choose safety every time
they will never know sublime.

June's Long Days

It's been a long day
has a different meaning in June.
Timelessness.
Each day,
longer than the one before
but not long enough for me.
The excess of light defies the dark
and I see I am not alone.
I toss aside my lanterns
and I wait for the dragonflies to appear.
My bare feet tingle as newness
sprouts up beneath them,
untainted and unspoiled.
The air smells of possibility,
possibility I want to believe.

Meeting Up with Second Chance

How could I have not seen you
when you first came around?
Was I too busy collecting remorse
to notice you looking right at me
and pointing in the direction I needed to go?
I might have sneaked a fleeting look at you,
but you came at the wrong time,
my throat having been constricted by shame.
Now I wait for you with breath bated,
looking around every corner
as if in those corners I'll find
what should have left my lips long ago.
But when I encounter you again,
I'll face you with an open mouth,
ready to reclaim my voice
and speak the words emblazoned on my tongue
for more than a decade:
Forgive me.

Twilight

It signifies many things:
a slow slipping below
or a rising just above,
a 'not quite'.
Between the light and darkness
that encloses my life.
Halfway there to anywhere or nowhere,
where I've been before.
Transition; it is, it is not.
I am, I am not.
Lost and found and lost again.
A before and after,
but far too fleeting to know the difference.
Approaching an end
that leads to a beginning
and a beginning that fades
like a final breath.
Neither daybreak or nightfall
and the quest for a conclusion of my own.
The glow of diffused light
that illumines my duskiest thoughts.
A midpoint.
A surrender.
The in-between
that never ceases to exist.
Twi-life.

Signs of Life

My moment of solitude
is disrupted
by a pack of children
playing outside my window
interlopers
shrieking
no worries
as if the world
weren't on fire
raucous, insufferable
cries of unreasonable joy.
It takes me a minute
to realize I'm not really angry.
I am envious.

So Many Ways to Hide

Behind the pages of fiction or fantasy,
plagiarizing the lives of others,
basking in their sun.
In your car, tinted windows
cloaking the blasphemous cigarette
and the thick tongues of long held tears.
Underwater, soundless,
unobserved by human eyes,
digging in the clam flats
or searching for that flawless shell,
wishing you had gills.

History

You whisper to me,
which isn't so bad.
You shriek at me,
and I become the eternal listener.
You shame me, the worst of all.

You follow me everywhere,
my perpetual companion,
draping me with your darkness
like a cloak whose weight will
drop me to my knees.
You beat on my ears with stories
of old and though I burned
your pages long ago
they appear in technicolor
from your bottomless crypt.
You wake with me,
demanding my attention,
even if it's soundless regret.
You repeat yourself
over and over,
as if I need reminders
of the shadows that tremor
on the screens of my life.

And when I finally seek slumber
in the silence of night,
I crave your absence,
but you never leave.
And you never sleep.
My perpetual companion,
you never sleep.

Tethered

You can't have one without the other.
It's impossible.
They are inextricable.
They have equal weight,
mighty weight,
but weigh nothing,
promising a lifetime of attachment.
They begin and end together,
sharing a common path,
circling one another in perpetuity
on the edge of a dizzying cliff.
I know them well,
like I know the sunlight
bright on water.
Love and loss,
tethered always.

Unrecorded Lives

In every life
there's a moment of greatness,
never witnessed, never celebrated,
no turning of heads or nods of recognition
or applause that resounds
in the halls of fame.

This may not seem like a tragedy
to most, but isn't it?
Aren't all lives
worthy of documentation,
at least in some small way?

The grandmother, with clouded eyes,
placing a bowl of soup
before her only grandchild;
the farmer, smelling of earth
and the sweat of animals;
the rest room attendant,
other people's messes
becoming her own;
the fisherman, weathered
by a lifetime of storms let loose;
all of them,
never to enter the vaults of history,
their light unable to shine
in the absence of human reverence,
like a log that won't burn
without a leaf to light it.

To all of them I want to say:
Tell me your story
because I know you have one.
Tell me the extraordinary things you've done.
Tell me everything, and I will record it.
I will place your words respectfully
on blank white pages
that will one day come alive in print
and reach the eyes and hearts
of multitudes,
where a poem is meant to go,
where your story is meant to go.

About the Author

Barbara DiMauro is a clinical social worker. *On This Earth* is her third book. *Not Always Sorrow* and *Celestial Conversations* were published in 2021 and 2023 respectively, both by Antrim House Books. Her poem "The Swamp Queen" was nominated for a Pushcart Prize. Her extensive travel, passion for the natural world, and political activism have greatly influenced her work. She lives on the Connecticut shoreline with her husband and animals.

www.ingramcontent.com/pod-product-compliance
Lightning Source LLC
Chambersburg PA
CBHW031204160426
43193CB00008B/498